PERENNIAL WISDOM

FILMS BY THE AUTHOR

India and the Infinite
Requiem for a Faith
Islamic Mysticism: the Sufi Way
Christian Mysticism and the Monastic Life
Buddhism: the Path to Enlightenment
Buddhism, Man and Nature
Zen and Now
The Flow of Zen
Flowing with the Tao
The Art of Meditation
The Mood of Zen
Taoism
Trip to Awareness: a Jain Pilgrimage to India
The Evolution of a Yogi
Living Yoga
Bali: the Mask of Rangda
Sacred Trance in Bali and Java
Meditation: the Inward Journey
The Ultimate Mystery
Life After Death
Biofeedback: the Yoga of the West
The Therapeutic Touch
Holistic Health: the New Medicine
Psychics, Saints and Scientists
How to Change the World
The Hundredth Monkey
Hinduism and the Song of God
Reflection: A Metaphoric Journey

PERENNIAL WISDOM

Unity in the World of Faith

ELDA HARTLEY

AMITY HOUSE
Amity, New York

Calligraphy: Miki Leeper
Interior Design: Elda Hartley
Cover Art and Design: Ernie Haim
Symbols drawn by Page Nall

ISBN: 0-916349-09-8

Published by Amity House Inc.
106 Newport Bridge Rd.
Warwick, N.Y. 10990

Printed and bound in the
United States of America

To

Peter Lagemann,
a fellow seeker,
in gratitude.

· CONTENTS ·

· FOREWORD ·

'The perennial philosophy'
forms the esoteric core
of hinduism, buddhism,
Taoism and christian
mysticism, as well as
being embraced, in
whole or in part, by
individuals ranging
from spinoza to ein-
stein, schopenhauer
to jung, william james
to plato.

the founders and true saints of the great religions have explained this esoteric core using different language, metaphors and emphasis: judaism - 'if i ascend to heaven, thou art there; if i make my bed in hell, behold! thou art there.' christianity: 'the father and i are one.' hinduism - 'atman (individual consciousness) and brahman (universal consciousness) are one', buddhism - 'look within, thou art the buddha', islam - he who knows himself knows god.

this common thread
inspired both this
present book and the
film, "the perennial
philosophy." perhaps
this approach to the
wisdom at the heart
of all the great spirit-
ual traditions will
take us one step
closer to understan-
ding our planetary
neighbors and, ulti-
mately, to world.
peace.

ELDA HARTLEY
COS COB, CONN.
1985

Time never was
when I was not
nor ever will be
when I am not.

Some see me
   one with themselves
   or separate;
      some bow to the
      countless gods
            that are
my million faces.

I am
the sire of the world,
and this world's
mother
and grandsire.

I am the end of the path
    the witness,
    the Lord
    the sustainer;

I am the place of abode
    the beginning
    the friend
        and
    the refuge.

I award to you
the fruit
of your action.
I am the heat of the sun;
the heat
of the fire
am I also.

I am the beginning
the middle
and the end
in
creation.
I am the divine seed
of all lives.

I am
your
True Self.

Taoism

As a Taoist I contemplate
nature's ways
and learn to move
as the fish
that swims
with the current
or the knife
that slips
with the grain.

The brooks and birds
the mountains and
forest
fill me with
constant delight,
but my joy is not ended
when grief rushes in,
because
there is no dark
without light,
no up
without down,
no bad
without good.

15

It's
yin and yang —
opposites
coming together,
creating a

whole.

I toss out
attachment to wealth
and unneeded possessions
since
life's physical needs
are not hard to come by.
My wealth comes
from wanting no more
than is needed
for
life's support.

17

How lovely this forest spring,
no one else within miles,
            just clouds
        of misty spray
            above
    the plunging torrent.
I climb toward the peak
& rest on pebbled bank
        and just enjoy
        each moment
                as if
    it were
            the last.

青蓮歌蜀道難易進
地說若卿與東坡莎逆群
巧拙癡心未退脱盡思縱笑
无請誰盡中人墜若此
青万山松雪才枝莉戌
叫絕　甲申年書藥作
龍趙萬懃

雲中子橋坊天外散峯青
甲申自擬元州老人法
井二祁

Though pent for years
within this world
of dust,
I neither work
nor worry
leaving all to nature's plan.

With nature's way
and man's
I'm really not concerned.
I do not scorn belief
in immortality
nor yet the priests
who seek
that kind of goal;

But were I asked
how best to cultivate
the Way,
I'd say:
Trust the Tao
and flow with it
while you till the mind
and tend the body well.

Judaism

O, God,

how can I know you?
Where can I find you?

You are as close to me
as breathing
and yet as far as
the furthest star.
You are as mysterious
as the vast solitudes
of the night
and yet as familiar
as
the light of the sun.

24

If I ascend to heaven
thou art there;
if I make my bed
in hell,
behold,
thou art there.

You can never be found
through thoughts,
only through love.

You learn about love
by loving,
and the more I love
the more I learn.

Wherever I aspire
to dreams
binding me to others,
wherever I open myself
to prayer ...
there will I find you,
for everyone is
a high priest
and every hand
stretched out
to friend or stranger
is an altar.

The search for you
    is full of dangers
and wrong turns,
but if I press on
    the wrong turn
    finally becomes
    the right turn.

The place to start

is

where

I

am.

The Book says,
"Hear, oh Israel,
the Lord your God
is
One God."

The sages repeat,

"God is One,
God is One."

No matter how desperate
my lot,
how deep the valley
of the shadow of death,
I do not lose heart,
because
the opportunity
for creative response
is
always
there.

People talk
of the coming messiah.
They think that you are
out there,
not in here.
You have taught me
that everyone
is a messiah,
and good deeds for one hour
in this world
are better
than all the time
in the world
to come.

If you are one
    then love for you
and for my fellowman
    go hand in hand,
because life is one.
Thus it is inevitable
    if my life is
        to be
    fulfilled,
that I love my neighbor
    as myself.
    with my heart
    not just my head.

Hinduism

As a Hindu
   I am free
from 'I' and 'mine',
   accepting pleasure and pain
   with equal tranquility.
If I am lucky
   I do not rejoice;
if I am unlucky,
   I do not weep,
neither longing
   for one thing
nor loathing its opposite.

When I know that my
essence
is the essence
in all creatures,
I become united with
Brahman,
cut free from
the fruit of the act.
Were this not so
I would be prisoner
enslaved by action,
dragged on by desire.

I make my own future
with every single thought.
This is Karma
a spiritual law.
    Pain or pleasure,
    love or hatred,
        poverty or wealth –
whichever I have,
it is just a reflection,
    an echo.

The truely wise mourn
neither for the living
nor the dead,
for there never was a time
when I did not exist
nor you,
nor is there a future
in which we shall cease
to be.
It is only maya, illusion,
that makes us imagine
that we are separate
and finite.

Worn-out garments
are shed by the body,
worn-out bodies
are shed by the dweller
within the body.

Not wounded by weapon,
not burned by fire,
   not dried by the wind,
      not wetted by water,
   not shaken by adversity,
      not hankering
      after happiness;

free from fear,
    free from anger,
free from desire,
    such is Atman,
    the soul ~

    such am I,
    your Inner Self

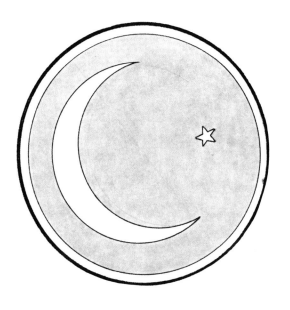

Islam

I am the soul of souls.
Not knowing
how near I am,
people seek me far away.
They are like him
who,
in the midst of water,
cries out in thirst.

I am
neither
wind nor fire,
water nor dust,
neither self-existent
nor created.

My station is without
space,
my mark
without impression.

I am the distance
of two bow-lengths
around the throne:
I am in all lands,
in all people,
at all times.

I am the Gospel,
the Psalter,
the Koran,
I am invisible
and omnipresent.
I am forever listening
but seldom speak.
I am a guiding hand
and a watchful eye.

I have many names
and many faces.
I am the part of you
that no one takes away.

I am that voice...
a voice that is heard
in the longest silence.

I know that I am
infinitely perfectable
and that the treasure
I seek
derives from work ...
work as vocation
and self-work,
the alchemy
whereby
we become perfected.

47

I know that within myself
there is an element,
activated by love,
which provides
the means of attaining
true reality,
of achieving
union with God
in this life
now,
not later.

As I spiral upward slowly
round and round
but each time higher,
I shed the illusions that
keep me earthbound
and take responsibility
for my future.

for I know that
the beginning
of the universe
is now –
all things are
at this moment
being created;

and the end
of the universe
is now –
all things are
at this moment
passing away.

Buddhism

The Buddhist in me knows
that suffering comes
from the wish to possess
and keep forever
things and relationships
which are
essentially
impermanent....

so I learn to be free
from attachment.

Attachment
to pleasure,
attachment
to loved ones,
attachment
to things,
and attachment
to the fruits
of my actions -

all these I let go,
and letting go
I gain all.

The ignorant
work
for the fruit of their action.
The wise work
also,
but without
thought of reward
and show how holy work is
when the heart
of the worker
is free.

I cannot find the Buddha
any celestial realm
until I have found
that
in myself
and other beings
as well.
I cannot find enlightenment
in hermitage cave
unless I find it also
in the
bustling marketplace.

I am the champion
of the middle way,
neither eating too much
nor fasting,
neither sleeping too much
nor holding back the night,
often alone
but not a recluse.

I live in the Now,
for yesterday is a dream
and tomorrow
is a vision,
but today,
well-lived,
fills tomorrow with hope
and makes
past dreaming
richer.

No dualism
of heaven and earth,
natural and supernatural,
man and God,
material and spiritual
mortal and immortal,
for
ordinary men
are Buddhas.

You and I are Buddhas...
the task is
to discover it.

The mind is its own place,
  and of itself
    can make
  a heaven of hell,
    a hell of heaven.
Therefore,
    my first task is
  to master the mind...
      to know that
    this very earth
      is the Lotus Land
        of Purity,
  and this body is the
  body of the Buddha.

60

Christianity

As a Christian
I hear again
the same refrain.
The words are different
but the thoughts the same—
God is Love
God dwells within.

If God dwells within
then to recognize God
is to recognize
myself.
Let me remember this—
I am one with God.
If I am one with God
then you are one with God
and we are at one
with all our brothers
and our Selves.

Everyone
lives in me
and I live in
everyone.
I am most I
when I transcend
my boundaries
and am aware
of my participation
in a world beyond me.

My task is not
to seek for love,
but merely
to seek and find
all the barriers
within myself
that I have built
against it.

Love waits on
welcome
not on time.

As I move
through the corridors
of time,
I learn that
perception
is a mirror,
not a fact,
and what I look on
is my state of mind,
reflected
outward.

If hatred finds a place
in me,
my world is filled
with fear.
If I feel
the love of God
within,
I see a world of
love and mercy.
My own condemnation
injures me,
my own forgiveness
sets me free.

Forgiveness
makes change
        possible.
Old grievances
    damn the flow
        to new life,
and forgiveness
    breaks the dam.
Forgiveness frees
    the forgiver.

I am responsible
for what I think,
and what I choose to think
generates
what I do.

I am responsible
for what I see and hear,
and the sights
I choose to see,
the sounds I choose
to hear,
construct my belief
in what I am.

I receive
as I have asked.

Why wait for heaven?
It's here today.

The present
is
the only time there is.
The past is gone,
the future but imagined.

Let me
repeat those words
I've heard so often,
  what Jesus taught
and showed...

God is Love,
God dwells within.
I recognize God in you.
  I recognize God in me.

In this way we are one,
we are in communion,
The harm I do to you,
I do to myself.
The love I give to you,
I give to myself.

God is Love
God dwells within.